RHYME TIME

Dec 19, 2020

RHYME TIME

Marcus,
Thank you for your
purchase.

Marc Blakeley

Marc the Shark

Copyright © 2020 by Marc Blakeley.
YouTube Channel : MarcTheShark Rhyme Time
Email Address: marctheshark86@aol.com

ISBN:	Softcover	978-1-6641-4360-9
	eBook	978-1-6641-4359-3

All rights reserved. No part of this book may be reproduced or transmitted in any form or by any means, electronic or mechanical, including photocopying, recording, or by any information storage and retrieval system, without permission in writing from the copyright owner.

Any people depicted in stock imagery provided by Getty Images are models, and such images are being used for illustrative purposes only. Certain stock imagery © Getty Images.

Print information available on the last page.

Rev. date: 11/24/2020

To order additional copies of this book, contact:
Xlibris
844-714-8691
www.Xlibris.com
Orders@Xlibris.com

821949

Contents

Chapter 1. What is Rhyming and How to Rhyme

What is Rhyming? 1

Chapter 2. Some Inspirational Poems

Damn Corona Virus 5
Its 5:30 in The Morning 6
Our Father God 7
Life is Hard 8
A Moms Love 9
House Cleaning 10
Mother Natures Fearful Wrath 11
If A Dog Had A Voice 12
I Wake Up Find Myself on The Shore 13
I've Gotten Off The Path 15
Almighty Father in Heaven 16
Save Me from My Crazy Foolish Odyssey 17

Chapter 3. Someone Special in Your Life

There is Nobody Else 21
Your Eyes, Lips, and Body 22
You Make Me Happier 23
Everytime I Look in Your Eyes 24
Im a Lucky Man 25
Baby Take My Hand 27
I Been on The Hunt 28

Embracing You 29
I Wish You Where Here...31
I Wont Make Plans... 32
The Chemistry We Had Blew Up 33
Let Me Show You One Time 34
Should I Continue to Chase.................................... 35
I wish 36

Chapter 4. Request

Yearly March 39
Little Bitty Worm.. 40
New Holland Tractors...41
Nothing Like A Harley Davidson 42
A Tall Simple Structor... 43
2020... 44

Chapter 5. Exes and Hoes

Im Glad were Done..47
Letting Our Love Go 48
I Hurt You, You Hurt Me.. 49
You Too Faded Away... 50
These Hoes are Scandelous......................................51
I Don't Even Want You Anymore 52
Ghost 53

Chapter 6. Random Rhymes

Yall Never Heard of Me 57
Its almost 4 a.m 58
Marc The Shark Coming Out After Dark 60
Is it Me or The Mirror 61
What are You Suppose To Do 62
My Rhymes are Vulgar 63
You Aint Nothing But a Petty Bitch 64
I Tried to Be Faithful 65
Im Really Nice and Sweet 66
Do You Know What its Like to be All Alone 67
My Eyes Stay Low 68
Marc The Shark from The 318 69
4:20 70
What Can You Do 71
Im Not Ghetto 72
Ill Have You Lying on The Mat 73
Ill be Causing Cyclones 74
S.B.C. is Where Ill Be 75
Marc The Shark is Back Again 76
Ill Rhyme About Anything 77
Going Down South 78
Weed Fiend 79
If I was Single 80
Some Real Sh*t 81
My Fighting Song 82
Punch Your Throat 83
You Put Me to The Test 84
Strappin, Packin, and Ready 85
Remember My Name 86

By The Time I Get Through 87
I Eat Pussy Like A Fat Kid Eats Cake 88
Far from The Same 89
Friday Night 90
Smokin All Day and Night 91
Ballin Hard 92
9 millimeter 93
Sittin here Fameless 94
All I Need 95
I tried 96

CHAPTER 1

WHAT IS RHYMING AND HOW TO RHYME

What is Rhyming?

Rhyming is when words sound alike

Example: the word sun rhymes with the words run and fun

HOW TO RHYME
An easy way to rhyme is to pick a word and change the first letter of it and see what it makes.

Example: For the word DEAR you could change the "D" to "N" and get NEAR. For the word FUNNY you could change the "F" to an "H" and get the HONEY or to an "M" and get MONEY although spelled different sounds the same.

Chapter 2
SOME INSPIRATIONAL POEMS

Damn Corona Virus

4-2-2020

Im sick of this damn corona virus

Im going crazy like Miley Cyrus

Bored looking at these same walls

Tired of walking up and down these same halls

In dire need of changing of the scene

Getting cabin fever if you know what I mean

Movies and tv quickly grow old

Thank God I don't have this death cold

Im happy my family and loved ones are healthy we are good even though we are not wealthy

When times are harder then most

Believe in the father, son, and holly ghost

Lean on them and they will get you through

Have faith in them and they will protect you

Its 5:30 in The Morning

—Its 5:30 in the morning I wish I was snoring

I'm tired but my brain is wired

tossing and turning one minute freezing the next minute burning

I wish sleep would hurry and come
let's get up and have a shot of rum

—I'm not worried about fame and glory, I just want to have enough money so I don't have to worry

I believe my rhymes can get me there
if you like them feel free to share

Our Father God

Our father God is number one.

Next is the Holy Spirit and his Only begotten son.

Known as Jesus Christ, only one sacrifice,

he died for our sins on the cross,

all he ask is for us to love and believe in him at all cost.

God grants miracles when they are needed most

believe in him and the son and the holy ghost

When times are rough pray for strength

with God's protection you can go to great length

LIFE IS HARD

Life is hard. it will leave you physically mentally emotionally scarred. but don't let that stop you even times are tough and you're feeling blue you have to pull through keep your chin up because one day will be blessed because you passed Gods test

A Moms Love

A moms love for her son, so solid should never come undone
Her love is endless pure and divine, she will come to his aid at the first sound of a whine

A love so strong it's a bond that cant be broken
even with the harshest of words spoken

House Cleaning

House cleaning can be a pain but it is worth the effort because of the gain

Walking into a sparkling Room That you just dusted and sweeped with a broom

The aroma of freshness in the air makes you happy and fades your despair

Your hard work has paid off you can enjoy a clean home no more germs or bacteria to make you sick or cough

Mother Natures Fearful Wrath

Mother nature you came from the Oklahoma skies, you took numerous innocent lives. My heart goes out to the families and cries. You came sudden without warning, now those families are mourning. My tears for their families are pouring. You destroyed everything in your path nothing stood a chance now everybody is cleaning up your aftermath. Mother nature why did you have to show your fearful wrath? Destruction and chaos is what you created your power and strength was underestimated. Lives and homes were lost, you came with great cost.

If A Dog Had A Voice

Id a dog had a voice he would ask if he had a choice if we could go out back to play with his toys or If he can go to the dog park and play with his boys

He will Say he loves you He Will say that he will be there even when your blue He will Say that he will be loyal through-and-through

He will say he is your best friend he will be by your side till the very end He'll say just love me and play with
And feed me and I'll be happy as can be

I Wake Up Find Myself on The Shore

I wake up and find myself washed up on the shore.
I check myself for injuries I'm not sore.

I call out for help but don't hear a sound,
I look in every direction I look all around

I see a tall orange and white tower I climb it to get a better vies,
I see a huge town I'm definatly somewhere new

While I have a minute to pull myself together, I take a bite of this apple I feel a little better.

As I'm walking through town just after sunrise,
Trying to gather supplies,
I hear this loud scream it caught me by surprise.

I look behind me, and I see a mother fuckin zombie!! So instinct I flee.

Weaponless and defenseless I hide in a shed, I'm sitting here thinking inside my head

Wait him out he will go away, so I hunker down and wait here until it turns day.

I am thirsty and hungry now in the middle of the night, I'm going to go look for some food and water I should be alright

...never to be heard from again,
He parished due to dehydration
rest in peace amen.

I've Gotten Off The Path

I've gotten off the path and now I'm lost. I need to find my way back at all cost. So I hit my knees and I pray please lord guide my way for my family's sake I'm sure their worried sick and wide awake so please Lord guide my way

Almighty Father in Heaven

Almighty father in heaven goes by many names i can think of at least seven

Jesus, Yashua, Christ, lord master, heavenly father, Son of man

He will wash away your sins with the blood of the lamb

He will grant miracles when needed the most

Believe in the father son and the holy ghost

For our sins he died on the cross,
hes our savior and master, he died like a boss.

Pray to him he will hear
Sometimes it may seem like hes nowhere near

But have faith he will soon come
Be patient on our time his clock doesn't run

Save Me from My Crazy Foolish Odyssey

The girl here is always full of excuses
each one pulls on my heart strings like a bunch of nooses

Are they Logical or all lies
Are they facts with a disguise

Don't play games keep it real
Don't say you guna do shit then change the deal

Please dear Allow me to kindly retort
From now on I am putting in no more effort

If you want me come find me maybe we could be Even though your face is all i ever see You probably won't come save me from my crazy foolish odyssey

Chapter 3
SOMEONE SPECIAL IN YOUR LIFE

There is Nobody Else

There is nobody else in this world id like to get to
know more about than you

I wana know you more and more each passing
day boo

I want us to know each other through and
through

I'm an open book with no secrets or lies
you can ask me anything your heart likes

I will always be honest and 100 percent true

So go head ask me anything it could be the first
thing that comes to mind or anything else will do

Do you mind if I ask you a question or two

Who is your hero and what is your biggest fear
What makes you angry and whats your favorite
time of the year

Your Eyes, Lips, and Body

You're eyes are as bright as a sparkling sapphire
So mezmerising hypnotizing im no liar
Your lips are soft and tasty as strawberries
Picked from the finest of prairies
Your body is like an hourglass curved in all the right places
When I see you my heart pounds and races

You Make Me Happier

You make me happier than I've been in my entire life.
I want you to know that one day I hope to make you my wife.
You made your way straight through to my heart smoothe as butter on a hot knife.

In my heart is where you will always stay.
My words are true with this I don't play.
I mean every word of what I say.

I'm yours always and forever
I feel like we were meant to be together
You make my soul feel free as a feather
I hope our intertwined hearts never sever

Im Walking around my mind is in a daze, it's only been a few hours since I seen your pretty face, but really it feels like its been a couple of days
Every second you are running through my mind, go ahead baby walk that line, I can definitely tell you are one of a kind

I can still feel you when I close my eyes, remember that feeling when I was kissing up and down your thigh? You got me feeling like that 24/7 for real Im telling no lies.

I'm so addicted To you
I will always stay true
I can tell your addicted to me too

Everytime I Look in Your Eyes

Everytime I look in your eyes, my tummy get butterflies. I get this tinglin feelin. My nerves are doing anything but chillin. I would walk for miles just to see one of your smiles. They brighten my day. Theres no more gray, hey what can I say? You got the body of a goddess your lookin so flawlessyour leaving the boys wide eyed and jawless. You're the perfect angel lookin at it from every angle my heart and your tangle

I'm a Lucky Man

I'm a lucky man to have you hold my right hand I am mesmerized by your pretty eyes your soul has me hypnotized and I tell no lies when I say the love bug bit me by surprise

You stole my heart and soul, I look forward to spending forever with you and together growing old.

I'm blessed that you're my girlfriend, I promise to be the the best man u ever have even after our worlds end.

Everyday I wake up with a smile, cuz all night your going through my mind like your running a mile

You are always on my mind, you are special and mean so much to be me Baby you are one of a kind

There is a girl from Louisiana her name is Savannah maybe one day we're going to be living like kings and queens in Havana

She stole my heart right from the start I really hope she never tears it apart.

I don't think she will
This girl is the real deal
We go great together just like jack and jill

You are a dream come true, I've spend my entire life looking for a lady like you.

Each day that passes by, I like you more and more and that's no lie.

I am excited to see what our future holds, let's see how our relationship molds,
im gunna make sure you are happy everyday so it never folds.

You are perfect in every way, I want to be with you everyday.
So take my hand let's run away, We can go where ever you say.

BABY TAKE MY HAND

Baby take my hand and we can run away, we can run as far and as long as you say.
baby take my hand everythings gunna be okay, I'll be by your side till the very last day.
Baby take my hand we can laugh and play, we will be together that's what I say.

I Been on The Hunt

I been on the hunt to find the the most perfect girl that's a friend
One to knock my socks off and rule the world together till the very end

I'm looking for one that will faithfully love me and not play any type of head game
Stick together even when we drive each other insane

Its tragic though because a lot of them are all the same
They love to point the finger at you and give you all the blame
Never taking responsibility for their mistakes its really a shame

Ive walked for miles down this Rollercoaster of a road walked for years in solo mode

One day soon the hunt will will subside
One day soon will be the day I have her by my side

My journey might have come to an end
I think I might have found that one perfect girl who is a friend

EMBRACING YOU

Embracing you it's a dream and prayer come true
I never thought we would be kissing and making love too
I forever want to continue to do things we do
O know we both wanted this for a long long time
Im so glad our hearts have a chance to entertwine

I know you are not mine
But I'm all yours till the end of time

I will always be here for you I will do anything you ever ask me to
I want to see you happy because you deserve it
I will always keep you and your heart safe I will preserve it
I want that special spot in your heart can I reserve it?

Maybe too soon for you to know for sure
But I will patiently wait for you and I will never deter

You are truly an angel to me you are truly an amazing sight to see
I am truly persistent and sometimes to pushy

You are in every thought from the time I wake up till the time I go to sleep
My feelings for you are strong and they run so so deep

I dont know the distance my feelings and I should keep
So Im going for it all taking a giant leap

Im sure you already know how I feel so telling u shouldn't be that big of a deal

This is all for you and I'm keeping it 100 percent real

I want to be your friend your protector your lover and care for you and the kids till the very end

I know your independent and you don't need me
But I just want to be there and make you happy as can be

I Wish You Where Here

I wish u were here right now. heck,
Id look you in the eyes
id nibble on your neck
work my way down to your thighs
a few seconds later youd get a sweet surprise

I Wont Make Plans

I won't make plans. I will leave that in your hands. Just call me 30 minutes before. Ill get ready and walk out the door.

Come here or meet me there either way I don't care
its all up in the air
If we go out and get lit we can call uber for ride share

The Chemistry We Had Blew Up

The chemistry we once had went up and exploded
Does she want to start back from ground 0 and rework the formula or does she consider it Corroded

I am sorry things blew up i wish I could travel back in time to undo my screw up

Unfortunately though that is too bad. you can't change the past once you ruined what you had

Now the only thing you can do is shape your future
Hope these wounds you can suture

Surely all hope can't be lost i gota try to heal her wounds I caused gotta try at all cost

Possibly by trying im further causing more damage
But I can't let it be this way I must fix this I will manage

She is perfect in every way I will let her know hw special she is everyday

I hope her heart i can regain and the way things were can remain

Let Me Show You One Time

Let me show you one time.
I swear you're gonna wanna be mine.
I'm gonna lay it down like no other.
You're gonna ask to be my baby's mother.
I'm going to eat that pussy so fire. you're gonna be climbing the bed higher and higher.
My tongues gonna do some things. making you go insane. calln my name. havin you go off the chain.
I'm guna be loyal. we could be royal. you and me, ill be your king and you'll be my queen. ill provide everything you need know what i mean?
Let me show u one time. I swear your guna wan be mine.

Should I Continue to Chase

Should i continue to chase or should i slow down and give you some space
Sorry i am a really fast runner and i wana win this race but we can continue our current pace

The race to the finish line to when I can call you mine
I wanted this victory for a very long time

I dont want to beat you and i dont wana to lose we should have a tie so the winner could be both you and I

I WISH

I wish I wasn't unwanted you are all that I wanted

I wish your image would leave my head unhaunted

I feel the sting in my heart as each day passes with no word

You once made me feel light as a feather and free as a bird

No I'm in shackles waiting for you to come around

Im staying true to my word to you I will always be bound.

Questions arise more and more each day
here's what the thoughts in my head say

How long must I wait?
Did I do or say something that you hate?
Did I say or do something that didn't make you feel great?
When again can I see you?
Do you even want to see me too?
What can I do to steal your heart?
I wish we could spend every day Together and never have to part.

Chapter 4
REQUEST

Yearly March

Cute Silky black and white friend

To the world your known as a penguin

You love the freezing cold

Your yearly March with other penguins is really bold

You travel for months to find your one true lover

One day you will reunite with your son, his brother, and their mother.

You truly have a heart of gold
You will search for her till your dead and old

Humans are not that loyal
I want to come live with you on that artic soil

Little Bitty Worm

Little bitty worm
I see you squim it's raining, it's pouring, let's get you out of this mean old storm

Little bitty worm this can only be short term
Here is a tiny box to keep you warm

New Holland Tractors

New Holland tractors
You are Used in certain factors

To the world your massive and big
You can dig, bury, and cary a big load on your rig

Your mighty and powerful such a handy power tool

There are no limitations your used in many situations man that's cool.

Nothing Like A Harley Davidson

Nothing like a harley davidson such a powerful machine

When its engine roars that fucker sounds mean

Nothing like a peaceful ride
Taken in the country side

Miles and miles go by with the wind in your face

Nothing like taken a 10 mile cruise going your own pace

A Tall Simple Structor

A tall simple structure it can be a mile long or just a smidge it can separate you from your destination im taking about a bridge

Underneath could be traffic or a lake sometimes a walk or a swim you may have to take

It separates cities and people and other land
With a tiny stroll across you can be on the beach in the sand

2020

It's 2020 better stack your money
Some crazy Shits going down its not even funny

you better put your mask up cuz the worlds been gased up

Be smart be bold but don't catch the death cold or you may not live to grow old

Coughing and gagging the death cold runs deep in their veins
Covid 19 took over
And there is no cure nothing but pains

Is it a disaster or a man made death cold? theres theories but the truth remains untold

CHAPTER 5
EXES AND HOES

Im Glad were Done

Fuck You bitch I'm glad we're done

Go go go you better run

I'm done with your shit
Everyday you throw fit

I won't don't this anymore
You arrogant infant whore

Stupid bitch You make me sick
You can fuck off and suck my dick

Now your dead to me, ghost
I hope you like your little roast

That stupid bitch got mad and ghosted me. My anger took over uncontrollabley.
I said some mean shit i will admit I had a drunken fit.

Letting Our Love Go

She's so stupid for letting our love go, I can't believe she would act like a stupid little dumb hoe not taking responsibility, blaming it all on me, stupid little dumb hoe, this is all your fault don't you see. Stupid little dumb hoe if you wouldn't have ghosted me I wouldn't have roasted you stupid dumb little hoe I've done let u go

I Hurt You, You Hurt Me

I know I hurt you and you hurt me too everyday since then has been dark and blue

You mean the world to me and I ruined everything you and I were guna be

I let the alcohol and anger over come my senses and wasn't thinking straight don't you see

And I want u give u the most
sincere apology and I hope you can truly forgive me

I want us to be together forever like we had planned. Im sorry I turned into a horrible mean old man

But a relationship takes two and I know the damage done may be too great for you

I ask you to give us one more chance to see if this can become another once in a lifetime romance

I love you and I miss my honeychild this whole breakup is stupid emotions got wild

this much is true never again will I intentionally hurt you

You Too Faded Away

U too like every one else in my life faded away

You no longer say hey
or see what's happing my way
or ask to chill and play
But I don't give a fuck
you and everyone in this world suck

Maybe I'm to crazy or fucked in the head
Just for wishing sometimes I was dead

I just needed a friend
Thought u were guna be my best till the very end

But you vanished must have been some shit i said never that did i
Intend

My bad for fucking up that friendship we once had
Kinda sad kinda mad but fuck it will just put a smile and pretend I'm glad

These Hoes are Scandelous

These hoes around here are all some motherfuckers

Scandalous, Lying, cheating ghosting fuckers, playing games, plotting against us suckers

But bitches that ain't cool
I ain't the one play like a fool
Not guna let you use me like a tool

Now I know better then to give you my heart
You will be locked out from the very start
Never again will I be broke down part by part

Games and lies, I will see them in your eyes
spot them before you even realize
No more sleepless nights and endless cries

Fuck off every on of you lying, cheating, playing, Scandelous hoes

Yall make me sick like toe jam between the toes

I Don't Even Want You Anymore

I don't even want you anymore
you stupid game playing little whore

I thought you were my angel but really you are the devil in disguise

No longer will you pull the strings on my heart I sever all ties

Ghost

You say I'm being too persistent and pushy and you need your space

Your wish is granted ill give you all the distance you need cuz my time ill no longer waste

You ghosted me for the last time
So for you I got a little rhyme

Go play with someone else's head

U shouldn't be a ghost unless your dead

Go waste some one else's time

im done trying to make you mine

But I really did care about you and wanted you more than words can ever explain

I tried to contain. but these feelings they pour out they're too hard to restrain

I tried to get past your guarded walls
but you just keep breaking my balls

It seems to me
You're not the girl
I knew from before,

You turned into quite the little whore!

Lying and stealing my heart ♥

Blowing me off like a fart!

Fuck you!
You god damb tart!

All I wanted was a beautiful girl

But you didn't want to give it a whirl.

When you're all used up,

Standing on the corner with your cup,

I'll walk by with my prize on my arm,

Then you will say darn!

You had your chance

Now you missed the dance.

I wanted to be your host,

Instead you were just a ghost.

Ride another weiner and a different tongue,

The dinner bell has rung!!!☐

Peace im out

CHAPTER 6

RANDOM RHYMES

Yall Never Heard of Me

Yall never heard of me
but that's about to change because my words a murdering
my killer rhymes are making news headlines
marc the Sharks going to be everywhere even in The Times
my name is going to reach you
My words are going to teach you
if you talk shit
I'll make a fist and brutally beat you
Haters I don't care if you don't like me
I'm right here come and fight me
I'll kick your ass then steal your Wifey

Its almost 4 a.m

It's almost 4 a.m. and I'm not tired.so I toss and turn, my body feels wired. Got a million thoughts on my mind like you were the perfect find. I want you to be mine, I'll be here for you until the end of time. I want to hold you close and kiss you gentle, all this thinking can drive a man mental. I'm going to close my eyes and try to sleep, brain you must be quiet now, not another peep

I wish your lips were mine, I am glad that our hearts have intertwined, you brighten up my day you make my world shine, you are so beautiful and yet so fine, I'll always be yours as long as you are mine.

You are perfect in every way, I want to be with you everyday. So take my hand let's run away. We can go where ever you say. So come on this adventure and let's have fun and go play.

I know we've only just met, but you are the most perfect girl yet, i can tell were going to get along just fine.

We don't have to rush things we can take it slow, my heart beats faster at every thought of you just so you know.

I'm being 100% honest and not putting on a show.

You just give me the topic, and I'm gunna drop it. its gunna be so atomic, my flow will blow, and can't nobody stop it. my words will hit you like a drop kick. if we going to these hoes house, we got to drive quick. make sure you got your hoe, or she'll be on my dick. I'm gunna pull her so slick, I'm gunna be the one she pick. Cuz no man can compete with this tree branch I call my stick

I don't give a fuck about none of these hoes they can all suck my cock as it grows imma bust a nut on your face stomach and on your nose

Marc The Shark Coming Out After Dark

Marc the shark coming out after dark
Don't cross the boss or shits gunna start
I got my nine pointing your way
Locked and loaded and bullets ready to spray
You better duck you might make it out today

Is it Me or The Mirror

Is it me or is it the mirror?
Everytime I look in, my image gets a lot less clearer
Im standing infront staring,
my reflection changes into a thousand faces glaring.
Its like im on acid
a thousand images flashin
right infront of my eyes
not knowing who you are can make a grown man cry

What are You Suppose To Do

What are you supposed to do when you're sick of being single and can't find a good loyal girl whose down to mingle? I don't know what's going on with these stupid hoes, they can go fuck themselves as my cock grows they ain't shit they can't fuck with my flows they all wearing those skanky clothes lookin like a model who blows always with the drama they ain't ever gunna be my baby mama

My Rhymes are Vulgar

My Rhymes are vulgar they're hitting you like a boulder but if you need a cry I have a shoulder
I feel these Rhymes in my bones all my songs are going to be on everybody's ringtones
Don't treat me like No Hoe or your life will Flash and Go right before your eyes I tell no lies cross me and you could be the first person who dies

You Aint Nothing But a Petty Bitch

You ain't nothing but a petty bitch you ain't nothing but a way for me to scratch my itch when I feel like dog and I want it raw you're the one I call bitch you don't mean shit to me I'll fuck you, your sister, and every girl in this vicinity

I Tried to Be Faithful

I tried to be faithful and every time that was a no-go I tried to be respectful and every time that was a no-go I'm tired of these games I can't take it no mo from now on all these bitches going to be treated like a side hoe like a side hoe

Im Really Nice and Sweet

See I'm really nice and sweet I'll massage your feet or cuddle just like a teddy bear I'll give you all my kisses with plenty to spare

Do You Know What its Like to be All Alone

Do you know what it's like to be alone? when you have nobody and you're on your own? I wish I had me somebody to talk to on the phone. It's depressing I'm letting it be known. I want me girl to spend forever with and i want our relationship to grow. Don't want me a girl whose a trick or hoe.

MY EYES STAY LOW

my eyes stay low, cuz I'm smoked out fasho. I'm so high, im flying in the sky, watching clouds go by.

Marc The Shark from The 318

Marc the shark from 318 coming at you like an earthquake, gunna make your whole body shake when i hit you in the jaw you gunna be in awe spending the rest of your days eating through a straw. Cuz you won't have no teeth to chew both your eyes will be black and blue don't come at me or ill make your worst nightmare come true

4:20

It's a day, it's a time, when it comes by, you know im getting high. Ima be Smoking all day and night, busting sick ass rhymes till sunlight. ima come down but definitely not tonight. 420s my favorite holiday. call up the weed man tell him to come my way. bring a ounce of your best hay, we smoke nonstop all day.
come on by come get high you don't have to pay

Im far from same. as all the other white boys in this game. ima step to this mic and out em all to shame. because I can flow harder than the rest. watch me rip these rhymes just put me to the test. if you think I don't belong. I'll soon show that yall are wrong. My words are gunna hit u like a shot gun shell. Your gunna feel them very well. my lyrics are hotter than lava. they'll put an end to ur saga. Don't shed no tears or make a peep. My words are the reason reason your losing sleep. You can't get em out your head. your going crazy thinkin bout the shit I just said.

What Can You Do

What can you do when you like someone who cant be with you. Except tell them how you feel maybe they feel the same way too. But they are happy and unavailable at this time. You were too late to be that guy. But you don't want to interfere and you never want to see her cry. So I'll just let hese feelings hide and bide my time. Maybe one day she will be mine, but if not I'm happy to see her shine.

IM NOT GHETTO

Im not ghetto, but im going to serve these rhymes up like some shrimp alfredo.
Im a white boy with a bad ass skill.
Ill rhyme all day boy my rhymes are ill.
Haters don't fuck with me or some blood might spill.
I dont want to hurt you
And i I definatly don't kill.
But for real heres the deal.
I can rhyme about anything just name a topic.
Ill flow and blow up so hard it will be catastrophic.
Ill rise to the top and cant nobody stop it or top it, if you try, im guna flip flop it, and your face is gunna mop it

Ill Have You Lying on The Mat

Ill have you lying on the mat flat on your back and as your blood starts to pour I look at you and ask if you want some more you answer no because you know you cant go another round cuz youll get your ass knocked right back down

Ill be Causing Cyclones

Ima be causing cyclones when I throw my bows you better duck or ill break your nose have you bleeding out it just goes to show don't treat me like a ho or your life will flash and go right before your eyes tell no lies cross me and you can be the first person who dies only if you test me though I got my nine cocked loaded and ready to blow

S.B.C. is Where Ill Be

S.B.C. is where ill be Shreveport bossier city is where you can find me ill be smoking my herb chillin by curb if you wana step up just say the word youll get the bird and you keep walkin cuz I know ur scurrd

Marc The Shark is Back Again

Here we go Marc The Shark is back again. Hit my weed and your head will start to spin will make it last all day with just a twiny twin twin. Its that one hitter quitter its known in town as that hard hitter, its twice as vicious as jack the ripper just ask the hooker and the stripper

Ill Rhyme About Anything

Ill Rhyme about anything, I sure will, let me tell you the deal, I'm going to keep it real, and let you know how I feel. My rhymes are ill, on the mic I kill, I lay these rhymes down from dusk till dawn, yall will remember my name long after I'm gone.

Marc the shark yah that's my name. I'm on my game, on the road to fame. Ill put all these wanna be rappers to shame, and yeah I can hang with lit wayne. His rhymes are insane but mine get stuck in your membrane.

Going Down South

I want u to suck my dick
You can gag but don't get sick

Let the cream fill your mouth I love when you go down south

I love going down south too
I'll eat your peaches til they release that tasty goo
I'll eat them till your legs shake like an earthquake
But this you knew

Weed Fiend

Im a weed fiend and I don't give a fuck just a good o boy from Louisiana always down to buck I smoke the best trees if you think ima mess with anything less. Boy please. Ima get it no matter what the cost cuz that's how I roll cuz ima motherfuckin boss

If I was Single

If I was single
I'd mingle in the club. I'd see these hunnies, spending all their moneys. Dancing and getting drunk. I'd try to decide., which hunny id fuck. Tonight's the night to make one of these hunnies lucky. Hell ya! She even sucky sucky

Some Real Sh*t

Im guna spit some real shit, not about shootin niggas or spics, or goin to the country store and hittn them licks. Ima white boy you see, I ain't no G. I don't go around killin people in town. But I do gotta gat, so you better back down. Naw im just playin but watch out though no what im sayin? My girl is faithful unlike your ho wholl fuck anything she sees, you should go get her checked out for some s.t.d.s. hell she probably has some unknown disease

My Fighting Song

This is my fighting song, I'm comin at you strong. I see the end soon in sight. Im comin at you with all my might. Here it comes, you better hold on tight. Im guna smash your throat, then smash your face, then watch your teeth go all over the place. Now your lying on the mat. Slap on your back and your blood starts to pour. I look at you and ask... do you want some more? You answer no. because you already know, you cant go. Not even one more round cuz you'll be the victim of another beatdown.

Punch Your Throat

Im guna punch your throat
then watch you choke,
then write your momma a note.
Im guna tell her why,
her only son had die.
He messed with the wrong man,
and I killed him with one hand,
sorry but you understand.
I no its crucial and ruthless
but I wasn't guna be the one to end up toothless.

You Put Me to The Test

You put me to the test I turned out the be the best
I wasn't scared like the rest I put two in your chest
You took your last breath
cuz I just brought you to your death.

Strappin, Packin, and Ready

Marc the shark is always strappin, packin, and ready, to chop you up with my machine just like Jason did to freddy I got my nine ready to put a whole in your head, chest, and spine. If you run away youll get one in your behind. So take it like a man and don't whine, accept that its your time, count to 3 and everything will be just fine

Remember My Name

Im gunna rip these beats from dusk till dawn, yall are gunn remember my name long after im gone.

By The Time I Get Through

By the time I get through yall are gunna know my name im gunna be king of this rap game ima come up and things are gunna change I wont have to count no change ill have a cash flow with unlimited range im going to be buying and spending and and spending all this money im getting ima have a garage full of cars packed to the ceiling ima be with my homies just smoking and chillin.

I Eat Pussy Like A Fat Kid Eats Cake

I eat pussy likea fat kid eats cake
Wrap your legs around ill make your body shake

Gotta be Tasty
Can't be too hasty

Oo I love sweet Poontang pie

My tongue will work all day and night and that's no lie. I live to satisfy.

Far from The Same

Im far from the same. as all the other white boys in this game. ima step to this mic and out em all to shame. because I can flow harder than the rest. watch me rip these rhymes just put me to the test. if you think I don't belong. I'll soon show that yall are wrong. my words are gunna hit u like a shot gun shell. Your gunna feel them very well. my lyrics are hotter than lave. They'll put an end to ur saga. Don't shed no tears or make a peep. My words are the reason reason your losing sleep. You can't get em out your head. your going crazy thinkn bout the shit I just said.

Friday Night

Its Friday night we don't give a fuck

It's Friday night we bout to get buck

Its Friday night we bout to get Crunk

Its Friday night a we about to get drunk

It's time to toast so raise your up cups
all my smokers roll up your buds

Its Friday night and it's going down

smokers light them blunts n pass em round

Fill them mugs up to the rim
that liquor in there makes me grin

pop open the next bottle of that jim and here we go again

Smokin All Day and Night

Ima be smoking all day and night ima be smoking till I can't stand up right ima be smoking weather you think it's wrong or right if you don't like it come on let's fight
Your going to need to smoke after I get through making your eyes black and blue your gunna want about a pound of that bag of Mr. magoo
Ita make you see straight it will make you feel great better prepare for the munchies go make some cup cakes

BALLIN HARD

Ima be ballin hard. Cruising down Barksdale boulevard. got my gun in my waist cuz im always on guard. don't try to test me or you'll get scarrrd.

9 MILLIMETER

Nine millimeter semi-auto. just got paid like I won the lotto. going to the strip club and guna papa Hundred Bottles. then goin to the swim party with all the models.

Sittin here Fameless

I'm sitting here fameless my lifes anything but painless I feel like it it's going to get better cuz im a go getter

I hear the fame from the rap game is dangerous but I don't know cuz im sitting here fameless I laugh in the face of danger watch it tho cuz I'm quick to anger I always got my nine so don't try to come at me or I'll shoot off your wanger

All I Need

All I need is my jim beam and my sack of weed

They numb the pain also keep me from going insane

Day to day my skies are dark and gray
Depressed stressed nothing goes my way

So i say fuck it
2 tears in a bucket

Lets get wasted and pass this day away

Hopefully tomrrow will be a better day

I TRIED

I tried to be sweet and nice
But that didn't suffice
So now I will be a dick and act like a prick this is the attitude u decided to pick

CPSIA information can be obtained
at www.ICGtesting.com
Printed in the USA
FSHW011032051220
76461FS